CW01460483

WITHDRAWN

CELEBRITY SECRETS

TV CELEBRITIES

ADAM SUTHERLAND

WAYLAND

First published in 2011 by Wayland

Copyright © Wayland 2011

Wayland
338 Euston Road
London NW1 3BH

Wayland Australia
Level 17/207 Kent Street
Sydney, NSW 2000

All rights reserved.

Editor: Julia Adams
Designer: Stephen Prosser
Picture researcher: Julia Adams

Picture Acknowledgments: The author and publisher would like to thank the following for allowing their pictures to be reproduced in this publication:
Cover and 17: Huw Evans/Rex Features; cover (background graphics): Shutterstock; 1 and 19: Rex Features; 2 and 14: Shutterstock; 4: Jonathan Hordle/Rex Features; 5: Barbara Lindberg/Rex Features; 6: Tim Rooke/Rex Features; 7: FremantleMedia Ltd/Simco Ltd; 8: Rex Features; 9: Geoffrey Swaine/Rex Features; 10: WireImage/Getty Images; 11: Getty Images; 12: WireImage/Getty Images; 13: FremantleMedia Ltd/Simco Ltd; 15: Getty Images; 16: Nils Jorgensen/Rex Features; 18: Getty Images; 20: Allstar Picture Library/Alamy; 21: FremantleMedia Ltd/Simco Ltd; 22 (top): London Entertainment /Alamy; 22 (centre) Jonathan Hordle/Rex Features; 22 (bottom): Nils Jorgensen/Rex Features; 23 (top): Allstar Picture Library/Alamy; 23 (centre): David Fisher/Rex Features; 23 (bottom): Shutterstock; 24: Shutterstock

British Library Cataloguing in Publication Data:
Sutherland, Adam.
   TV celebrities. – (Celebrity secrets)
   1. Television personalities–Biography–Juvenile
   literature.
   I. Title II. Series
   791.4'5'0922-dc22
ISBN: 978 0 7502 6565 2

Printed in China

Wayland is a division of Hachette Children's Books, an Hachette UK company.

www.hachette.co.uk

Contents

Richard Hammond

Richard was nicknamed 'Hamster' by his fellow Top Gear presenters, because he is small and hairy!

Richard's car collection includes a Ford Mustang, a Morgan V6 Roadster, a Porsche Carrera S and a Ferrari 550.

Stats!

Name: Richard Mark Hammond

Date of birth: 19 December 1969 in Solihull, Warwickshire

Education: Richard went to Ripon Grammar School in North Yorkshire, and then to Harrogate College of Art and Technology, before starting work as a presenter on local radio.

Best Known For: Racing – and crashing – cars (*Top Gear*), and blowing things up (*Blast Lab* and *Brainiac*).

Big Break: Richard was presenting one day a week for satellite TV channel Men & Motors when he got the opportunity to audition for *Top Gear* in 2001. Along with Jeremy Clarkson and James May, he was chosen as one of the presenters for the show's relaunch.

TV Shows: Highlights include *Top Gear* (2002–present), *Brainiac: Science Abuse* (2002–06), *Richard Hammond's Blast Lab* (2009–present), *Total Wipeout* (2009–present), *Richard Hammond's Engineering Connections* (2009–present), *Sport Relief* (2010).

Secrets of his success: Richard is always bubbling over with enthusiasm for everything he does – from racing dragsters to rating children's experiments.

Life Story

Richard is one of the most popular presenters at the BBC. But 20 years ago, he almost gave up presenting completely. He was making so little money as a local radio DJ that he had to sell his motorbike to afford to buy food!

He took a full-time job in public relations and stayed there for nearly 10 years until the opportunity came along to present a daytime car show on a small satellite TV channel. A year later, Richard had been chosen as one of the three presenters on the relaunched *Top Gear*.

The *Top Gear* presenters are not afraid to put themselves in danger for the show, and in September 2006 Richard survived a 314mph crash in a jet-powered dragster.

Top Gear is a huge international success, with an estimated 350 million viewers worldwide.

Incredibly, he was back on the show for the new series in January 2007.

Richard also presents the hilarious *Total Wipeout*, where contestants compete on a scary giant obstacle course, and most recently *Richard Hammond's Blast Lab* – a fun way to look at the best (and most explosive) bits of science. Richard loves his job!

Questions and Answers

Q How does it feel as such a car fan to present Top Gear?

A "It was [my childhood dream]. But I never take it for granted. I'm always terrified I'll be fired!"

Richard Hammond, *Sunday Times*, 2008

Q What was the idea behind Blast Lab?

A "I really wanted to make a science show for kids, which they could enjoy and get involved. You don't need to want to grow up and be a scientist. It's about understanding how and why things do what they do and how the world works. If [kids] can learn something by getting something blown up or someone covered in custard then they love that!"

Richard Hammond, www.femalefirst.co.uk, 2009

Konnie Huq

Konnie has a degree in economics from Cambridge University.

Konnie was a guest on *Blue Peter* at 14, singing a solo with the National Youth Music Theatre.

Stats!

Name: Kanak Asha Huq

Date of birth: 17 July 1975 in Hammersmith, London

Education: Konnie went to a private all-girls' school Notting Hill and Ealing High School in London, and then on to Cambridge University, where she studied economics.

Best Known For: Being the longest-serving female presenter on *Blue Peter* and for presenting *The Xtra Factor*.

Big Break: Konnie started her presenting career at 17, interviewing Labour Party leader Neil Kinnock for *Newsround*. After university, she saw a magazine ad looking for TV presenters. She went along and got a job presenting *Blue Peter*!

TV Shows: Highlights include *Eat Your Words* (1993), *Milkshake!* (1997), *Blue Peter* (1997–2008), *UK Top 40* (2002–04), *London Talking* (2007), *UK School Games* (2008), *Mind Your Language* (2010), *The Xtra Factor* (2010–present), *71 Degrees North* (2010).

Secrets of her success: Konnie is a good listener who tries to engage with the viewer and make her interviews interesting to watch. On *The Xtra Factor* (as she did on *Blue Peter*) she tries hard to connect with the people she is interviewing and make them feel comfortable.

Life Story

When she was 14, Konnie Huq was in the National Youth Theatre and appeared on stage with actor Jude Law. But Konnie, whose parents came to England from Bangladesh in the 1960s, realised there were very limited roles for Asian actors. So she decided to follow her back-up plan instead and study for a degree at Cambridge University.

Questions and Answers

Q Was it difficult to make the move from children's TV to more grown-up programmes?

A "If you watch me on *Blue Peter* and then on *The Xtra Factor*, I wouldn't say it was completely different. I'm just me and what you see is what you get."

Konnie Huq, *Heat* magazine, 2010

Q Were you nervous on your first day on *The Xtra Factor*?

A "Everyone knew each other so it was like the first day at school! But in next to no time I felt really welcomed into the gang and now I don't feel like the new girl at all."

Konnie Huq, *Heat* magazine, 2010

After university she landed a dream job in TV – co-presenting *Blue Peter* – and stayed there for more than 10 years. Konnie visited war-torn Angola, was an extra in a Bollywood film and, in her last ever show, broke a Guinness World Record by pinning 17 Blue Peter badges onto fellow presenter Andy Akinwolere's shirt in one minute!

Since leaving the show in January 2008, Konnie has appeared on a number of shows aimed more at adults, most recently replacing Holly Willoughby as the host of *The Xtra Factor*, ITV2's companion show to *The X Factor*. In July 2010, Konnie married TV presenter, journalist and critic Charlie Brooker in Las Vegas!

Konnie backstage at the X Factor interviewing the host Dermot O'Leary.

Harry Hill

AWARD-WINNING COMEDIAN

Name: Matthew Keith Hall

Date of birth: 1 October 1964 in Woking, Surrey

Education: Harry went to Cranbrook School in Kent, and St George's Hospital Medical School, before training in brain surgery at the University of London.

Best Known For: *Harry Hill's TV Burp* and *You've Been Framed*, both on ITV1. And for his bald head, high collar and big glasses!

Big Break: After four years presenting *The Harry Hill Show* on Channel 4, Harry moved to ITV as the star of *TV Burp*. The show has since won three BAFTAs and four British Comedy Awards.

TV Shows: *The Harry Hill Show* (1997–2001), *Harry Hill's TV Burp* (2001–present), *The All New Harry Hill Show* (2003), *Harry Hill's Shark Infested Custard* (2005–06), *You've Been Framed* (2004–present).

Harry has recently launched a range of Fairtrade peanuts called Harry's Nuts!

Secrets of his success: Dedication and lots of hard work. Every episode of *TV Burp* represents 10 hours a day of TV watching for a whole week to pick out the funny bits. Harry does all this research himself!

If Harry wasn't a comedian, he would like to be a painter. Go to his website to see some of his paintings.

Life Story

Harry Hill spent his childhood wanting to be a brain surgeon. Then, when he qualified, he gave it all up to be a comedian! Harry learned his trade doing stand-up gigs – where he developed his trademark 'glasses and suit' look – and gradually built a reputation as a genuinely funny new talent.

Harry won a Perrier Best Newcomer's Award at the Edinburgh Fringe Festival in 1992, and was offered a job writing jokes for BBC Radio 4's *Week Ending* show. The following year, the radio station gave him his own show, *Harry Hill's Fruit Corner*, and in 1997, Channel 4 asked Harry to rework *Fruit Corner* for a TV audience. *The Harry Hill Show* ran for four years and established Harry as a TV regular.

Harry at a signing for his book, *Livin' The Dreem*, a comedy autobiography.

Questions and Answers

Q **Can you remember your first performance as a stand-up comedian?**

A "I had all my jokes written on my hand. I did the first, it got a laugh – and it completely threw me. I'd rehearsed it in front of a mirror – bang, bang, bang – and hadn't allowed for any laughter!"

Harry Hill, *Big Issue* magazine, 2010

Q **How do you make sure people will find your jokes funny?**

A "It does my head in! I have a little book and I write jokes down. Then I write a shortlist [of the best ones]. It's a bit like revision."

Harry Hill, *Big Issue* magazine, 2010

Since 2001, Harry has been presenting *TV Burp* – a comic look at the week's television, from soaps to dramas to reality shows. The show has been a huge success, regularly getting 7 million viewers, and has won several awards. Harry also writes books, and has his own comic strip in *The Dandy*.

Holly Willoughby

Since joining ITV in 2004, Holly has presented everything from children's tv to chat shows.

Holly would like actresses Kate Winslet or Drew Barrymore to play her in a film of her life!

Stats!

Name: Holly Marie Willoughby

Date of birth: 10 February 1981 in Brighton, East Sussex

Education: Holly attended the private Burgess Hill School for Girls, and then The College of Richard Collyer in Horsham, West Sussex.

Best Known For: Presenting *The Xtra Factor* until 2009, and *This Morning* and *Dancing on Ice* on ITV1, both with Phillip Schofield.

Big Break: After four years at the BBC, Holly was asked to co-present ITV's big Saturday morning children's show *Ministry of Mayhem* in 2004. The show was the follow-up to Ant and Dec's *SMTV Live*.

TV Shows: Highlights include *S Club TV* (2000), *Xchange* (2000–04), *Ministry of Mayhem* (2004–06), *Holly & Stephen's Saturday Showdown* (2006), *Dancing On Ice* (2006–present), *Holly & Fearne Go Dating* (2007), *The Xtra Factor* (2008–09), *Celebrity Juice* (2008–present), *This Morning* (2009–present).

Secrets of her success: Holly's determination to succeed has been her greatest asset. At 19, she persuaded a friend to help her record a showreel (a video clip of her 'presenting' an imaginary TV show). The showreel got Holly her first agent and a contract with CBBC!

Life Story

Holly is dyslexic (a learning difficulty that affects a person's ability to read, write and spell correctly), and so was never a great success at school. However, at 14 she was spotted by talent scouts at *The Clothes Show Live* and was signed to Storm Models, who also represent Kate Moss. By the time she was 17, Holly was appearing in ads for companies like Pretty Polly.

Questions and Answers

Q What special skills do you need to be a TV presenter?

A "I can't sing, I don't play any instruments, I'm rubbish at jokes... But I can talk for England! Thank God there is a job in which I can do that for a living!"

Holly Willoughby, *Daily Mirror*, 2008

Q You've worked with Phillip Schofield a lot. Did that make it easier starting on *This Morning*?

A "There's a lot of body language that you learn to read, a lot of understanding of how that other person ticks on screen... Fortunately we already [had] that rapport after four years of *Dancing On Ice*. So... my first day on *This Morning* felt as though [I'd been there for ages]."

Holly Willoughby, *Telegraph*, 2009

Holly and Fearne Cotton promoting their Best Friends guide.

In 2000, she got her first break in television, appearing in a show starring the band S Club 7. When the series ended, Holly was lucky enough to get hired as a first-time presenter for a BBC children's show called *Xchange*. Holly worked at CBBC for the next four years, before moving to CITV to present *Ministry Of Mayhem*.

Since 2006, Holly has been working on family entertainment shows like *Dancing On Ice*. She has also written a book with fellow presenter and best friend Fearne Cotton called *The Best Friends' Guide to Life*. Holly and Fearne are currently two of the faces and guest designers of fashion website www.very.co.uk.

Dermot O'Leary

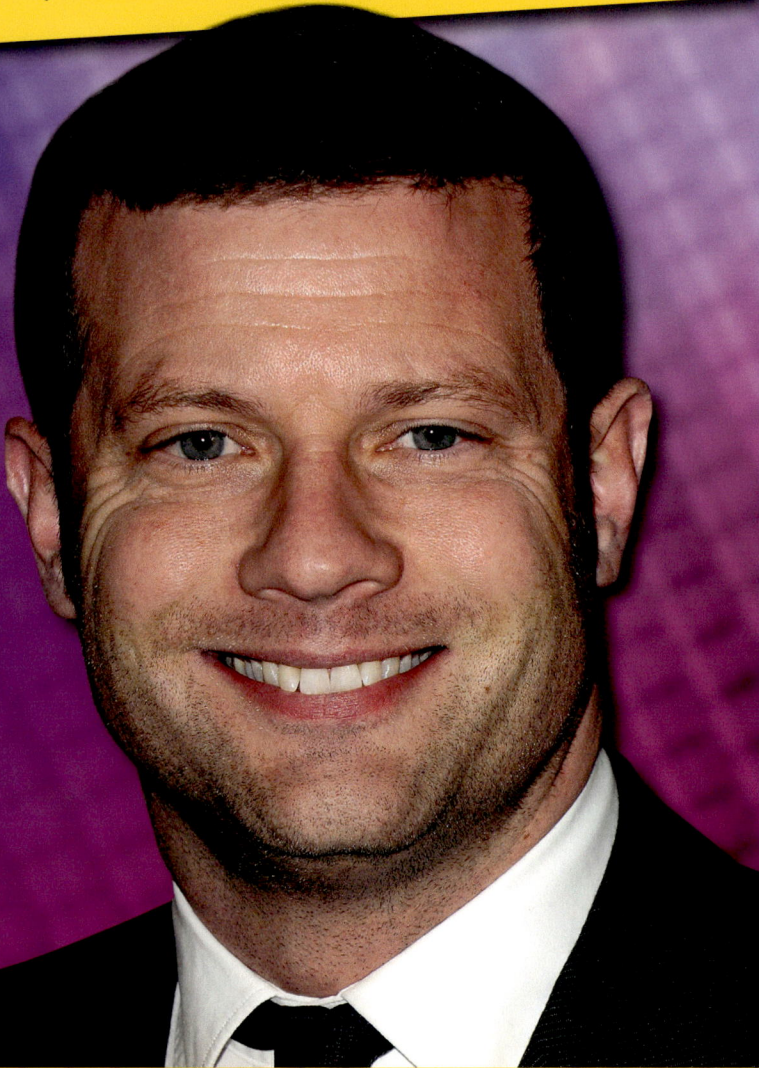

Dermot introduced Michael Jackson's final UK appearance back in 2009!

Dermot's childhood hero was Irish chat show host and *Children In Need* presenter Terry Wogan.

Stats!

Name: Seán Dermot Fintan O'Leary Jr

Date of birth: 24 May 1973 in Colchester, Essex

Education: Dermot went to St Benedict's College in Colchester, then on to Colchester Sixth Form College, before studying Media and Television at Middlesex University.

Best Known For: Presenting *The X Factor* on ITV1, and *Big Brother's Little Brother* on Channel 4.

Big Break: In 1999, Dermot went from production assistant on lunchtime comedy chat show *Light Lunch with Mel And Sue*, to being one of the original presenters on Channel 4's *T4*.

TV Shows: Highlights include *T4* (1999–2001), *Big Brother's Little Brother* (2001–08), *Big Brother's Big Brain* (2006–07), *The X Factor* (2007–present), *Big Brother: Celebrity Hijack* (2008), *The National Television Awards* (2010), *Soccer Aid* (2010).

Secrets of his success: Dermot is funny, confident without being bigheaded, and genuinely interested in the *X Factor* contestants he presents every week. He can front the biggest show on television and make every viewer feel like he's talking to them individually.

Life Story

Dermot O'Leary is one of Britain's most popular TV presenters, and fronts the UK's most popular show. The 2010 final of *The X Factor* had the highest viewing figures of any British TV show for the last nine years! And Dermot held it all together flawlessly.

An Essex boy born and bred, Dermot manages to achieve the difficult task of being popular with both male and female viewers. He makes you feel comfortable, shares a joke, pokes some fun at Louis Walsh and Simon Cowell, and makes the biggest show on television run as smoothly as clockwork.

Dermot interviews Take That singer Jason Orange during 2010's X Factor series.

Dermot's career has had its share of ups and downs. Out of university, he struggled to get his first break, sending out hundreds of applications, and going for dozens of interviews before getting his first job on *T4*. He soon became the golden boy of Channel 4, until *Big Brother's Little Brother* started losing out in the ratings to Russell Brand's louder, ruder *Big Brother's Big Mouth*. Then Dermot was chosen to replace *The X Factor's* original presenter Kate Thornton in 2007 – and the rest is history!

Questions and Answers

Q Why did you become a TV presenter?

A "I desperately wanted to work in television. I always say to children I meet, "Do you want to be famous?" If they say yes, I say this isn't the job for you, because that's not why you should be getting into [it]... As a presenter, you're working on behalf of the audience, [not yourself]."

Dermot O'Leary, *Marie Claire* magazine, 2009

Q Did you get recognised a lot more when you started presenting The X Factor?

A "I [went] from three million *Big Brother* viewers vaguely knowing who I am, to 10 million. They don't know my name, but they still point at me in the street!"

Dermot O'Leary, *Telegraph*, 2008

13

Cheryl Cole

Cheryl combines a hit music career with her role on X Factor.

Stats!

Name: Cheryl Ann Tweedy

Date of birth: 30 June 1983 in Newcastle upon Tyne

Education: Cheryl went to Walker Comprehensive School in Newcastle. From the age of nine, she also attended the Royal Ballet's summer school every year.

Best Known For: Being the biggest-hearted judge on ITV1's *The X Factor*, a Number 1 pop star and member of Girls Aloud.

Big Break: Simon Cowell asked Cheryl to replace judge Sharon Osbourne for the fifth series of *The X Factor* back in 2008. The show's huge success has catapulted Cheryl into the limelight as a true TV star.

TV Shows: *Popstars The Rivals* (2002), *Girls Aloud: Home Truths* (2005), *Girls Aloud: Off The Record* (2006), *The Girls Aloud Party* (2008), *The X Factor* (2008–present), *The Passions Of Girls Aloud* (2008), *Cheryl Cole's Night In* (2009).

Secrets of her success: Cheryl is warm, funny and, above all, caring. She understands what *X Factor* contestants are going through, and seems to live every emotion with them!

Cheryl's appearance on the ITV1 show *Piers Morgan's Life Stories* won 7.2 million viewers – the most in the show's history.

Life Story

Cheryl Cole is one of Britain's best-known and best-loved TV personalities. She grew up with her four brothers and sisters on a rough council estate in Newcastle and was suspended from school twice before leaving at 16. But Cheryl was always destined for stardom. She won Bonnie Baby contests, acted in TV ads, and was named World Star of Future Modelling at the age of six!

Questions and Answers

Q Have you always wanted to be famous?

A "I *never* wanted to be famous! What drives me is the desire to be successful, because what's the point of being a failure and famous?"

Cheryl Cole, *Glamour* magazine, 2009

Q Were you ready for the move to TV when you became a judge on The X Factor?

A "[No] I didn't feel ready, but [Simon] kept texting me and in the end I gave in. Simon is the most charismatic man I've ever met — it's like he's trancing you or something! It's actually quite scary."

Cheryl Cole, *Vogue* magazine, 2009

At 19, she entered *Popstars The Rivals* and became one of the founder members of the ultra-successful band Girls Aloud.

Since 2008, Cheryl has been one of the judges on *The X Factor*. The first two series she did, her acts – Alexandra Burke and Joe McElderry – won. But just as importantly, TV viewers enjoy listening to what Cheryl has to say about all the acts. A former reality contestant herself, she understands the ups and downs that go with the process, and is always there to give a pat on the back or a shoulder to cry on. There are rumours that Cheryl will be joining Simon as a judge on the US X Factor, which launches in 2011. If she does end up on the judging panel, she's sure to become a huge star across the Atlantic too!

Cheryl with 2010 X Factor finalists Cher (left) and Rebecca (right).

Matt Smith

Matt is the 11th actor to play the Doctor, the world-famous Timelord.

Matt auditioned for the part of Dr Watson in the BBC series *Sherlock*, but producers thought he was too similar to Benedict Cumberbatch, who played Sherlock Holmes.

Stats!

Name: Matthew Robert Smith

Date of birth: 28 October 1982 in Northampton

Education: Matt went to Northampton School for Boys, where he was voted Head Boy. He got 3 A-levels, and then went to the University of East Anglia where he studied drama with creative writing.

Best Known For: Playing the Doctor, the world's most popular time traveller.

Big Break: Matt was up against a lot of more experienced and famous actors when he auditioned for the main role in Dr Who. Nevertheless the producers loved his portrayal of the Doctor, and persuaded the BBC to hire him.

TV Shows: *The Ruby In The Smoke* (2006), *Party Animals* (2007), *Secret Diary of a Call Girl* (2007), *Moses Jones* (2009), *The Sarah Jane Chronicles* (2010), *Dr Who* (2010–present).

Secrets of his success: According to *Doctor Who* writer and producer Steven Moffat, the Doctor is a very difficult part to play. You have to be old and young, academic and an action hero all at the same time. Steven thinks Matt is the perfect man for the job!

Life Story

If a back injury hadn't halted Matt Smith's promising football career at just 16 years old, he might have been a Premier League defender, rather than a Timelord. Instead, he decided to throw himself into acting, earning a place at the National Youth Theatre, and then completed a drama degree.

Out of university, Matt started to win his first professional acting roles, including a part in the stage play *Swimming With Sharks*, alongside Hollywood actor Christian Slater. He quickly moved into TV, with back-to-back parts in the BBC adaptations of the novels *The Ruby In The Smoke* and *The Shadow In The North*.

Matt with his Doctor Who co-star Karen Gillan.

Questions and Answers

Q Why do you think *Doctor Who* is such a successful show?

A "It's the best ever TV drama format. It is not limited by space, time or genre. The Doctor can be reinvented in any way you like. Anything goes. Everyone wants to see this charismatic, alien, bonkers professor turn up and save the day. We'll never tire of that!"

Matt Smith, *Telegraph*, 2010

Q Do you get recognised a lot more now?

A "People come up to me 50 times a day! How do I deal with it? I wear a hoodie and a pair of shades and I keep my head down... [But] it's a small price to pay when you get to run around time and space every day!"

Matt Smith, *Telegraph*, 2010

Matt was a surprise choice among both viewers and critics when he replaced the very popular David Tennant – who was voted 'the greatest ever Doctor' – in TV's longest-running science fiction show. Fortunately, he has quickly won over the show's 10 million fans. Matt brings fun, youthful enthusiasm and a great mix of the brilliant and the bizarre to TV's most popular time traveller. He is a natural in the role!

Tess Daly

BELLE OF THE BALLROOM

A devoted mum, Tess has written a book on bringing up children.

Name: Helen Elizabeth Daly

Date of birth: 27 April 1969 in Birch Vale, Derbyshire

Education: Attended New Mills Secondary School and got nine O-levels, but left school to pursue a modelling career.

Best Known For: Co-presenting *Strictly Come Dancing* on BBC1 with Bruce Forsyth.

Big Break: Tess made a tape of herself interviewing a famous author and sent it to the producers of *The Big Breakfast*, who immediately offered her a slot on the show.

TV Shows: Highlights include *SMTV Live* (2002–03), *Back To Reality* (2004), *Sports Relief* (2004), *Strictly Come Dancing* (2004–present), *Make Me A Supermodel* (2005), *Just The Two Of Us* (2006), *This Time Tomorrow* (2008), *Children In Need* (2008–present).

Secrets of her success: Tess is warm and charming on camera. She is very good at putting viewers – and *Strictly* contestants – at ease.

> **Bruce Forsyth has given Tess the nickname 'Miss Sunshine' because she's always in a good mood!**

Life Story

Tess Daly was spotted outside McDonald's in Manchester by a model agent and flown to Tokyo as soon as she turned 18. At first she hated it, and cried every time she spoke to her family on the phone. Gradually, though, she started to pick up jobs and continued modelling around the world for the next 10 years.

Despite her success, Tess always wanted to be judged on more than just her looks, and was keen to make a mark in television. Her first home-made video clips earned her a job on *The Big Breakfast*, and from there she worked her way through music channels like MTV and Smash Hits TV, children's television, and onto Saturday night primetime with *Strictly Come Dancing*'s eight million viewers!

Questions and Answers

Q Did you enjoy working as a model?

A "As a model you are completely judged on what you look like... You can turn up on time, you can be professional, but at the end of the day if they want a blonde you're in, if they want a brunette you're out. As you get older you get more frustrated with that..."

Tess Daly, *The Scotsman* magazine, 2009

Q Do you get to keep all the great dresses you wear on *Strictly*?

A "[My daughters] would like to see me wear the dresses around the house. Sadly, I don't get to take the outfits home. They are just hanging in storage somewhere, gathering dust. It breaks my heart!"

Tess Daly, *Observer*, 2010

Tess, who is married to fellow TV presenter Vernon Kay, is now one of the most familiar and popular female faces on BBC1. The couple have two daughters, Phoebe and Amber. Tess has recently written a book, *The Baby Diaries*, and launched her own range of beauty products, The Daly Body Collection, with Marks & Spencer.

Tess shares a joke with Strictly co-host Bruce Forsyth.

Simon Cowell

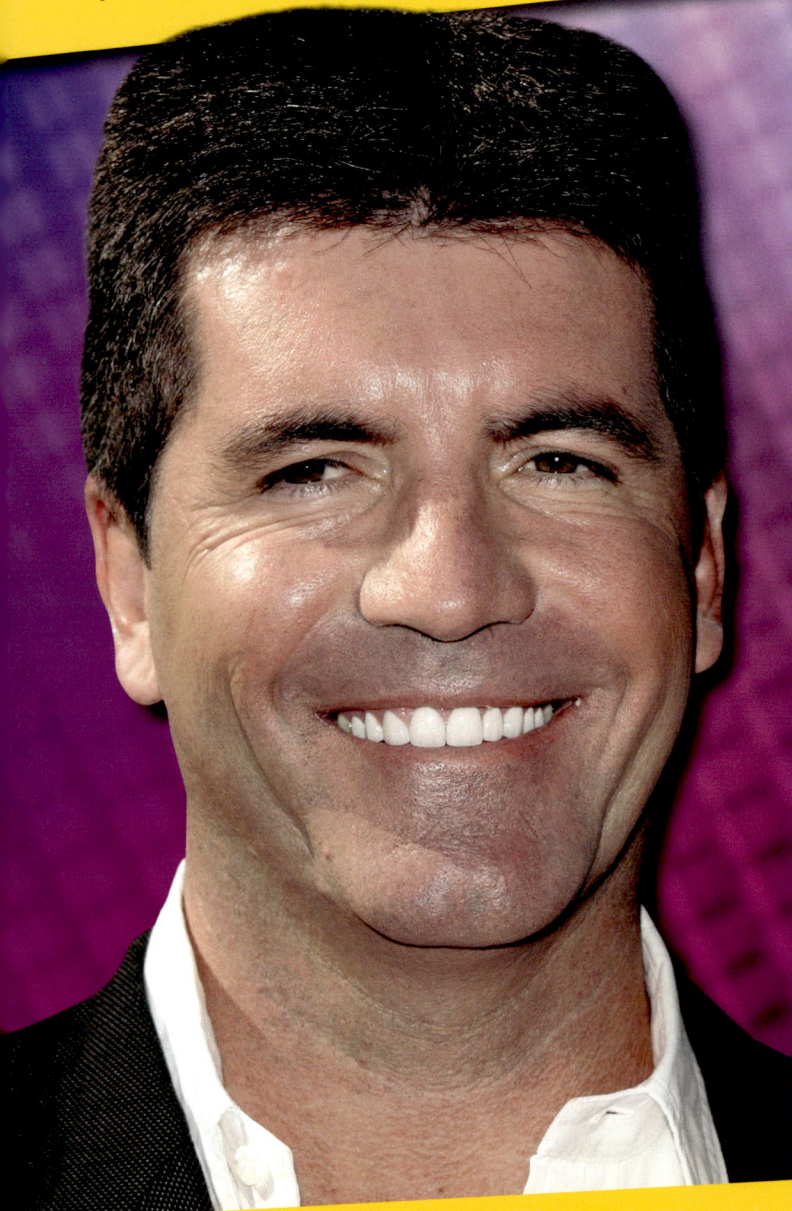

Simon has made an estimated £120m from hit TV shows like X Factor.

Stats!

Name: Simon Philip Cowell

Date of birth: 7 October 1959 in Brighton, East Sussex

Education: Simon attended the private school Dover College, but left at 16 when his dad got him a job in the mailroom at EMI Music Publishing.

Best Known For: Creating *Britain's Got Talent*, and the most successful show on British television – *The X Factor*.

Big Break: In 2001, Simon Fuller (the man who created the Spice Girls) asked Simon to be a judge on his new TV talent show *Pop Idol*. Within one series, Simon was the star!

TV Shows: *Pop Idol* (2001–03), *The X Factor* (2004–present), *Britain's Got Talent* (2007–present), *American Idol* (2002–10).

Secrets of his success: Since Simon first appeared on TV screens in *Pop Idol*, he has built a reputation for daring to say out loud what other people are only thinking! He started out as TV's 'Mr Nasty' but these days he is just as likely to praise a great performance as criticise a bad one.

Simon was paid **£15** million per series to be a judge on *American Idol*, making him the second-highest paid **US** presenter behind Oprah Winfrey.

Life Story

Simon Cowell spent 20 years in the music business as an unknown – but successful – manager of bands. In fact, he only started his TV career at 42. Since then he has created TV shows that are broadcast around the world, and he is one of Britain's richest men.

Simon became the judge everyone loved to hate. His favourite expression was 'I don't mean to be rude, but...' and he often brought contestants close to tears. Within a year, he went from *Pop Idol* to *American Idol*, and became a star on both sides of the Atlantic.

Simon with fellow X Factor judges (left to right) Cheryl Cole, Danni Minogue and Louis Walsh

Questions and Answers

Q **Did you ever imagine that *Pop Idol* would make you so successful?**

A "[Never.] I just felt instinctively that by using television as a vehicle we would have a better chance of selling records. [That] was the primary reason for getting involved, not wanting to get my ugly mug on TV."

Simon Cowell, *Observer*, 2008

Q **How has success changed your life?**

A "I looked at my diary [the other day] and realised I had the next 18 months planned! I could tell you where I was going to be every day – which city, what time... [I] can't escape it... I've got a responsibility to lots of people."

Simon Cowell, *Daily Mail*, 2009

At first, Simon was just a (well paid) judge on fellow music manager Simon Fuller's shows. But he quickly realised that there was much more money to be made by creating and producing his own shows! *The X Factor* and *Britain's Got Talent* became big hits, creating stars such as Leona Lewis, Matt Cardle and Susan Boyle. In 2011, he will finally be launching his own American version of *The X Factor*. Simon's success looks set to continue.

21

OTHER TV STARS

Christine Bleakley

Basic Information

Full name: Christine Louise Bleakley

Born: Newry, County Down, Northern Ireland

Birthday: 2 February 1979

Career, likes and interests

Background: Christine started working as a runner (TV assistant) and then floor manager while studying for her A-levels. She continued to work at BBC Northern Ireland while she took a politics degree, but left university before her final exams when she was offered a full-time job in TV.

Best known for: Presenting *The One Show* on BBC1 with Adrian Chiles and appearing as a contestant on *Strictly Come Dancing*. She became even more well-know when her and footballer Frank Lampard became an item.

TV shows: *The One Show* (2007–10), *Daybreak* (2010–present).

Big break: Christine had barely presented outside Northern Ireland when she was asked to co-host BBC1's *The One Show*. Viewers loved the show's format and the chemistry between Christine and Adrian Chiles. It became an instant hit.

Secrets of her success: Christine is ambitious, hard-working and always has a smile on her face!

Website: www.iTV.com/daybreak/presenters/christinebleakley/

Karen Gillan

Basic Information

Full name: Karen Sheila Gillan

Born: Inverness, Scotland

Birthday: 28 November 1987

Career, likes and interests

Background: Karen started acting at 16 at Edinburgh's Telford College. She went on to do a degree at the Italia Conte Academy of Theatre Arts in London, but dropped out to take her first acting role.

Best known for: Playing Amy Pond in the BBC1 series *Doctor Who*.

TV shows: *Rebus* (2006), *The Kevin Bishop Show* (2007–09), *Harley Street* (2008), *The Well* (2010), *Doctor Who* (2010–present).

Big break: Karen was working part-time in a pub when she was talent spotted for a modelling job for London Fashion Week. She spent two years modelling before working her way back into TV. She was invited to the *Doctor Who* audition, and found out the same day that she had got the part!

Secrets of her success: Karen is fearless, funny and ready to take on any challenge.

Website: www.karen-gillan.net/

Miquita Oliver

Basic Information

Full name: Miquita Billie Alexandra Oliver

Born: Paddington, London

Birthday: 25 April 1984

Career, likes and interests

Background: Miquita was brought up by her mother, the TV presenter and singer Andrea Oliver in London's Notting Hill. One of her best friends at school was singer Lily Allen. The pair would tell their parents they were having sleepovers at each other's houses so they could sneak out to warehouse parties!

Best known for: Co-presenting *Popworld* with Simon Amstell and presenting *T4*.

TV shows: *Popworld* (2001–06), *T4* (2006–present), *Miquita Does* (2009), *The Month With Miquita* (2010).

Big break: Miquita was still studying for her GCSEs when she landed the job presenting *Popworld*. The show mixed pop news with gossip, celebrity interviews, music videos and live performances.

Secrets of her success: Miquita is gutsy, has a sense of humour, and puts the enjoyment of the audience first. She has built a reputation for asking her guests unexpectedly cheeky or funny questions.

Website: www.channel4.com/t4/presenters

Gary Lineker

Career, likes and interests

Background: Gary was a professional footballer for clubs including Leicester City, Tottenham Hotspur, Barcelona and Everton. He is England's second top scorer (behind Bobby Charlton) with 48 goals for his country. He is famous for never having being shown a yellow or red card during his career!

Best known for: Presenting *Match Of The Day*, advertising Walkers Crisps.

TV shows: *They Think It's All Over* (1995–2003), *Match Of The Day* (1995–present), *Golden Boots* (1998), *Northern Exposure* (2009).

Big break: After retiring from football, Gary moved into presenting. He started on BBC Radio 5 Live, and joined *Match Of The Day* in 1995 as a regular studio guest. When Des Lynam moved to ITV in 1999 Gary took over as the show's main presenter.

Secrets of his success: Gary admits to spending a lot of time rehearsing for *Match Of The Day* broadcasts to make sure his links sound as natural and relaxed as possible.

Website: http://www.bbc.co.uk/pressoffice/biographies/biogs/sport/garylineker.shtml

Basic Information

Full name: Gary Winston Lineker
Born: Leicester
Birthday: 30 November 1960

Jack P Shepherd

Career, likes and interests

Background: Jack was a child actor who won his first TV acting role at nine! By the time he was 12 he had left school, and was receiving special one-to-one tuition in a '*Coronation Street* classroom' above his dressing room.

Best known for: Playing 'bad boy' David Platt in *Coronation Street*.

TV shows: *Where the Heart Is* (1997), *Clocking On* (2000), *Coronation Street* (2000–present), *Ghosthunting with Coronation Street* (2008), *All Star Mr and Mrs* (2010), *Grouchy Young Men* (2010).

Big break: Jack joined *Coronation Street* when he was just 12, replacing the actor Thomas Ormson. In 2001 he won a Best Young Actor award!

Secrets of his success: Jack's character David Platt is someone that *Coronation Street* fans love to hate. Oasis guitarist Noel Gallagher once said he'd love a part in the show, just so he could 'knock David's block off'!

Website: www.iTV.com/coronationstreet/characters/davidplatt/

Basic Information

Full name: Jack Peter Shepherd
Born: Pudsey, West Yorkshire
Birthday: 14 January 1988

Lea Michele

Career, likes and interests

Background: At eight years old, Lea accompanied a friend to a casting for the musical *Les Misérables* in New York. She decided to have a go herself and ended up getting a part!

Best known for: Playing high school geek Rachel Berry in the hit TV series *Glee*.

TV shows: *Glee* (2009-present).

Big break: After *Les Misérables*, Lea performed in several musicals, including *Spring Awakening*, which won her a Tony (American theatre award) nomination. The show was seen by *Glee* creator Ryan Murphy, who wrote the part of Rachel Berry especially for her.

Secrets of her success: Hard work! Lea works 14-hour days — filming, rehearsing, and learning songs and dances for the show.

Website: http://www.imdb.com/name/nm0584951/

Basic Information

Full name: Lea Michele Sarfati
Born: The Bronx, New York City, USA
Birthday: 29 August 1986